The Escape

A Collection of Poems by

Rayah

The Escape
Rayah

© 2019 Rayah
Cover image by SadistikShadow

Printed in the U.S.A.

ALL RIGHTS RESERVED. This book contains material protected under International and Federal Copyright Laws and Treaties. Any unauthorized reprint or use of this material is prohibited. No part of this book, or use of characters in this book, may be reproduced or transmitted in any form or by any means, electronic or mechanical, including photocopying, recording, or by any information storage and retrieval system without expressed written permission from the author / publisher, except for review and educational purposes.

This collection is dedicated to those who have supported me, my chosen family. I escaped because of you, and I am grateful for each one of you. Thank you.

This collection is also dedicated to those who have yet to escape and for those for whom these poems might resound. I hope you take courage.

THE ESCAPE

A mistake
Never forget
You're at my bidding
You ruined me
I love you
I can't stand you're that way
I didn't want you
I'll be here for you
Your money is mine
That's not yours
The choices aren't yours
Always me first
The decision is mine
Never said that
Faulty memory
I know what's best
About your body
About your food
About your friends
You're stuck with me
You have to be loyal
Thicker than water
Respect me
Serve me
You're crazy
Those are pipe dreams
You'll never make it
You need me

I danced
pranced
tiptoed
And glided
Under the radar
But you still sought me
You still bought me
By pulling fake proclamations from your pocket
To be taken at face value
Nevermind the broken promises
your favorite currency was guilt
Followed by fear
And control
they danced better
Through my head
And lead me through the steps
You gracefully maneuvered
Masqueraded by gaslit flames,
Scarring everyone who came close

One more
It was always one more...

Buying one more,
devouring
And digesting one more

Everyone knew,
And no one noticed.

Smuggling was easy
The car trunk...
Purses and bags...
On a shelf...

Escape lies within
Between the covers

4

You got it wrong
I didn't envy the blue, sparkly ballgown
It wasn't the glass slippers i dreamed about
Nor the pumpkin turning into a carriage
It wasn't the crown
The mice
The magic
Nor the prince
It was the bippity-boppity-boo
The rescue
The relief that can only come from breaking away
from those who had trapped and imprisoned me so long
I didn't want to be a princess
I wanted to be free

Push
Heave
Grasp
Breathe
Gasp
Next foothold
Next handhold
Feel
Scour
Explore
Panic
Slip
Next crevice
Small respite
Push
Inhale
Exhale
Don't look down
Only up
Next foothold
Next handhold
Scale it

6

I work and strive
For a man upstairs
Because tales of love
And threats of hell
I give everything
Yet he never shows
Nor writes
Only when we part
I find the light

"Lesbian"
Her voice stings
My neck prickles
A response demanded
I don't lie
Mostly I don't

She suspected
"Eve" comes a little too excitedly
off my tongue
And around my lips
Flutters around my middle
Lands red on my cheeks

I don't lie
Mostly I don't
There was Mark
And John
And Seth
I give her one of those,
It tastes stale on my tongue

8

A breath of relief
Tonight no barrage
no questions
Or not so subtle jabs
Night of solitude
Safe haven
Another day
Another story
The same walk in reverse.
Fate unknown

You kick up dust
That's been settled
Once before
And once again
We go 'round
Once again you
Knock me into the ground
Grasping for a hold
Trying to find the strength
No one wins
I cut you off
I walk away
But pain never fades

You, attention seeker
No longer get me
Because I'll be the one who escapes

Lift off
Plummet
Upswing
Collapse
Ever upward,
Onward
Day-by-day
Moment-by-moment
Intentions set
My wings grow stronger
Waiting for the moment the wind catches just right

I give
care
bend over
Never want to offend
hurt
Or scar
You call me sweet.
Gentle,
Kind

But that's not it
It's the nurture
Not my nature
a scared rabbit
threatened
Scooped up
The wolf on the prowl
Treat all with caution
With anxiety
Because… one wrong move
And you, too, may eat me

A warm bed, still tingling flesh
Groggy electricity in the air
We rest among the pleasure of the morning's dew
I stretch, rolling over to greet you
To kiss you once more
But you've already left me for Mr. Sandman
Back to back we lie
The sheets now cool
 familiar loneliness pervades

"Four weeks, get out"
Four fingers held out
A four word demand
Four letter words run through my head

They said it'll heal
But stitches never hold
Push in
Pull out
More holes
Rip delicate tissue
Push in
breath catches
Pull out
Choke back tears
Push in
Curl up
Pass out
Repeat anew tomorrow

The drizzle
Large glass drops
pelting the sidewalk,
Grass, buildings, benches,
Trickling down
Assailing all beneath
Translucent beads
Shattering upon icy impact.

Chosen family
We hold dearest
Not tied by blood
But by refuge
Wrapped in warmth
Safety found
As we hold each other
proud community resounds

Despite you
Pushing me down
Despite the years
And tears in misery
Despite the control
And guilt trips you spring
Despite your harassment
And daily ordeals
Despite the hell
You dragged me through
And especially despite you

I rise
And I fight
I rise
And I press on
I rise
And I survive
I rise
And prove everyone wrong
I rise
And I don't stop rising
I rise
And I soar
You don't own me
Not anymore

Some complain of butterflies
Anxious, excited flutters
But I have slugs
Heavy, squirming, slimy
Leeching out life

The heart can heal
After it is cut open
And scooped out
Grime scraped from its walls
Stitched delicately, patiently back together
And tucked back in
Behind, now fractured, armor
To wait for distant relief

A crowded lobby
Of the cautiously hopeful
Each with a thick stack
Of paper
Pages collected and compiled
to verify their worth
Make a case for hunger

The man in blue hovers
By the door
In the grimy lobby
He "protects"
waves of anxiety overtake
feelings of fraudulence

Stomachs rumble
The lady at window 2 calls
The file stamped
Sustenance gifted

Chance and circumstance
With a dash of effort
And a pinch of intention
A recipe to succeed

Double for woman
Triple for queer
Quadruple for dark skin
The recipe times five if two or more apply

Half the effort if wealth is added

The dust settles
The morning calm
And I rebuild
Brick by brick
Peace by piece by piece

A multitude of evil
Refined into a few simple words
Fuels the pen
The ink processes
Traumas and tragedies re-lived
The pages help cope with tortuous minds

Change doesn't come lightly
She knocks the door down
And grabs you by the shoulders
Shakes you awake
And makes you feel everything
Rarely taking no for an answer
Thrusting you into a new way of being
Jarring your senses
And rattling your nerves

RAYAH learned to read at age four and has been immersed in books ever since. She has a Bachelor of Arts in English and has published several smaller works in various anthologies and literary journals throughout her writing career, and she is excited to debut *The Escape* as her first stand-alone book. When Rayah is not working on her next writing project, you can find her enjoying life in Tennessee with her two roommates and their two adorable cats.

www.ingramcontent.com/pod-product-compliance
Lightning Source LLC
Chambersburg PA
CBHW030136100526
44591CB00009B/681